I0837763

Landlord Starter Guide

How to Survive as A Landlord in
The Age Of COVID-19

CONTENTS

The Age of COVID-19

In the absence of a vaccine, effective treatment or widespread testing, the age of COVID-19 is here to stay for the foreseeable future. Even if a vaccine were to be discovered tomorrow, your property as a landlord, commercial or residential, would remain affected.

Non-Payment of Rent

A significant number of legal jurisdictions are preventing evictions for non-payment of rent or any legal issues aside from violence during public quarantine periods. Tenants are taking advantage of this fact and not paying rent (even if they have the funds to do so because of government stimulus programs).

Many legal jurisdictions have also cancelled all in person eviction hearings, rescheduling them for dates far in the future when it is hoped the quarantines will be lifted or cancelling them entirely and rescheduling them as telephone hearings. This has had the effect of more than doubling the wait time for an eviction to take place. Prior to COVID-19 in most jurisdictions the delay between filing for eviction for non-payment of rent and obtaining a hearing was 1 - 2 months (you had to wait your turn). COVID cancelled all of the eviction hearings that were already backlogged. When the quarantine is lifted all of these hearings will be rescheduled in the order they were filed, increasing the delay from 1-2 months to 3-4 months in many jurisdictions. You must anticipate and understand this now. And understand that it will happen again if there is a second wave of infections and quarantine re-established.

Despite the fact that landlord applications about non-payment of rent are on hold in most jurisdictions, tenant applications about harassment or maintenance are not. Those applications are moving forward via telephone so the system is holding landlords accountable for maintenance and behavior while allowing tenants to do whatever they please while the quarantine persists. There exists no legal jurisdictions in Canada and few in the United States of a political character that will allow evictions during the pandemic for non-payment of rent regardless the circumstances and tenants know it. Many are organizing "rent strike" campaigns and planning to use this public health crisis as a cudgel with which to beat their landlords for the high crime of charging rent to use their space. These campaigns are going to be effective and receive the *political equivalent* of widespread support --- as tenant rights groups such as ACORN are simply better organized than small to medium sized landlords who are most affected by rental arrears and delays in evictions. Such organizations have already been effective in shaping the law to their benefit to an extent far outstripping small to medium sized landlords. There is also a widespread belief that landlords are being 'forgiven' mortgage payments by their lending institutions.

The accuracy of this belief is irrelevant, what matters is that it is widespread and affecting renters attitudes about withholding rent.

Even if you are prevented from evicting a tenant because of a quarantine period, serve the tenant the appropriate eviction documents and if necessary, file the application. You will be placed in a que in most jurisdictions which will begin operating once the quarantine period has been lifted. If you wait until the quarantine has been lifted to file your application, you will be severely behind in the que to have your case heard.

Eviction for a Purchasers Own Use (or any other purpose)

The freeze on evictions is also affecting renters who were scheduled to be evicted for a purchasers use of the property. For example, let's consider you have a condo you are selling that is currently tenanted. The tenant who occupies the rental unit does not want to leave (perhaps they are paying below market rent). You successfully sell the unit and the new buyer is moving in during a quarantine period. The Landlord and Tenant Board in Ontario, for example, will not evict the current occupant during a quarantine period. If you have a sale transaction closing during this time, you have most likely contractually promised the buyer vacant possession of the property. You will be on the hook for violating that contractual agreement. If you are a landlord selling tenanted property during COVID-19, ensure you have a clause in your Agreement of Purchase and Sale allowing for **significant** extensions to evict tenants if necessary. Also clauses which extend a transactions closing date until a quarantine period has passed. Tenants are well aware of the leverage they have been given because of this public emergency. Our office has had many landlords who have been extorted by tenants demanding $10,000 - $30,000 to leave a property that has been sold, knowing they can frustrate the sale of the property by delaying their eviction. This is widespread. This is real.

Inspection and showings to prospective tenants

Previous to COVID it was illegal for a tenant to interfere with prospective showings of a unit to potential purchasers or prospective new tenants. There were a multitude of ways tenants managed to do this anyway (refusing to put away large dogs, leaving the unit a mess, locking the doors or blocking access to areas of the home). Post COVID tenants are using the virus as an excuse not to allow the landlord entry into their own property. The claim will be that your presence, or the presence of any potential third party, is a danger to the tenant or the health of their children. This claim will be independent of the volume of PPE (Personal Protective Equipment) you are willing to wear or the schedule duration of the visit. When all safety protocols are followed such objections are not actually about safety they are about frustrating the landlord. During COVID quarantines you will not be able to evict for this purpose in most jurisdictions. But you should still file the appropriate paperwork including whatever appropriate filing fees. Ensure you document all your efforts to enter the home and make a compromise with the tenant. Follow whatever public health guidelines are proposed by public health in your jurisdiction. For example, if you have sold your tenanted Condo in Ontario and the tenant denies the Purchaser entry for an inspection, ensure you document in any notice of entry all of the safety measures that would have been taken:

- The purchaser will be wearing a face mask and gloves

- The time inside the home will be limited to 20 minutes

- No objects will be touched

- Limit the number of people inspecting the property

- No one with cold or flu symptoms may enter the property

Eviction tribunals have a civil standard, that means a balance of probabilities (50% +1). You must always have a mind to demonstrating that you are being reasonable. Tenants objecting to protection mechanisms that are over and above those recommended by public health authorities are eminently not being reasonable.

The death of Commercial Real Estate

If you are a landlord and own a significant amount of commercial real estate in your portfolio, prepare for significant vacancies. Tragedies have the tendency to accelerate trends which were already taking place. Retail commercial real estate was already following a downward trajectory as a consequence of online retail sales (Amazon, Walmart). This trend is being sharply accelerated. Further, many commercial tenants who are having their employees work from home for the first time will discover that not only is such an arrangement possible, but perhaps preferable. They will reconsider whether or not they require the same volume of commercial space. Many employees will begin working from home and never wish to leave (though some of course, the opposite). Those of you who are commercial landlords in the restaurant segment of the economy should prepare for massive rent arrears and income loss. Restaurant business plans are based on profitability per table (which breaks down to per square foot -- or how many tables you can squeeze into a space). In the absence of a vaccine, effective treatment or widespread testing, social distancing will become a social value. Business models developed pre-COVID will simply not be profitable with half the number of people in a restaurant. You will need to be creative with your space.

If you are a commercial landlord understand that collaborative spaces, cafeterias and meeting spaces in most large commercial companies are being closed to accommodate social distancing norms. Ensure you have excellent images of your space if you are advertising for vacancies. It is smart to 3D model your entire commercial offering and not terribly expensive. In this way, prospective tenants may view the property online and visits can be minimized.

If you are evicting tenants in this atmosphere, ensure it is as a last resort. Courts are closed or overwhelmed. Constantly Communicate with your commercial tenant if they are undergoing difficulty (as most are).

Life as A Successful Landlord

Lessons Learned the Hard Way

1. Presume every potential tenant is lying to you on their initial application.

Presume they are lying about their employment, their income, their rental history -- presume they are lying to you about their name. Everything must be verified. Predatory tenants are like sharks only instead of blood they are attracted to naïve landlords who think their tenants are their future drinking buddies or friends. I have lost count of the landlords who never made a copy of their tenants legal identification. How do you even know they are who they say they are? You'll find out the hard way when you try to send a collections agency after them and "*John John Johnson*" doesn't exist.

You must collect information you can use to try and detect duplicity before the tenant is living in your property. Once they have moved in, the legal system will not save you. Delays in eviction are unavoidable, particularly in the age of COVID. It will take MONTHS to evict your tenant, and the clever ones can delay it for a year or longer. Meanwhile in addition to collecting no rent they may be trashing your property or causing other issues.

Obtain sufficient information to verify employment, prior rental history, identity and banking information (where they bank). No exceptions. If someone doesn't want to give you this information, what does that tell you? You need names, phone numbers and addresses -- information you can independently verify yourself. <u>Ask them for a voided cheque. Even if they are paying you via e-transfer or cash</u>. You want to know where they rest their head financially. Why? So that if you need to garnish their bank account because they destroyed your living room, you can do it. There's no use in obtaining a successful Order saying some tenant owes you money if they quit their job and vanish. Many tenants in big cities change jobs frequently -- but not bank accounts. If they don't want to get you a void cheque or claim they don't have one, have them provide you with a stub from the bank for pre-authorized payment. If they ask why, just say it's for legal reasons. Make something up. This should not be a problem and is only a problem to tenants who do not want you to know where they bank. Now why do you think that might be the case?

2. Presume the references your tenant has provided are lying to you.

Everyone we have ever evicted from one of our clients properties have gone on to rent from someone else. Some of them have asked our clients for references before they leave. Many of our clients have happily given them those references in exchange for their expedited departure. If that horrible tenant is now foisted upon another unsuspecting landlord so be it.

The trick is being able to know when you are being fed lies by a reference. We've found a trick that works 90% of the time -- **misstate the facts to the reference when you are asking them questions.** For example, let's say you are verifying rental history. Countless tenants will just have a friend pretend to be their former landlord when you call. These friends will seldom be given sufficient detail to answer questions that are simple, but specific.

If on your rental application your potential tenant wrote that he lived with the prior landlord for 2 years, misstate the length of time on purpose. While talking to the "former landlord" you can say, for example, *"Steve put you down as his former landlord. He says that he rented from you for 4 years, correct?"* Fake references will usually say, *"Yes, that's correct"*, because they don't know what Steve wrote down on the application form and are usually just instructed to say he was a great tenant. Their fear will be that they are remembering the length of time he lived there incorrectly, not that you are misstating what is written on the application form. Enquire further, *"He says the rent was $1500 a month?"* When he wrote down that the rent was only $1100. The more inaccurate garbage this person confirms, the more likely the entire reference is fake or it's a landlord who will say anything to get rid of their problem.

Do this for all references. You think employers don't remember how much money their tenant is paid per hour? Or makes per year? When you're corrected because the reference was honest and genuine just admit it was a mistake and move on.

3. Be careful when using real estate agents to find tenants

In large jurisdictions where real estate is expensive, many agents make a living finding tenants for expensive properties. These agents are typically paid the first month rent as compensation for finding a tenant and as the rent in many of these jurisdictions is significant, the practice can be lucrative. The problem with this system is that the incentives are not properly balanced. There are virtually no repercussions for agents who do a poor job of screening potential tenants. Some of the worst cases we have ever encountered were brought to us by landlords who hired a real estate agent to find them a tenant.

As an example, one of our clients were an elderly couple who owned property in Toronto but had retired to Florida. Before leaving Toronto, the two had purchased a luxurious, 4 bedroom condo in the downtown core. The condo was fully furnished and marketed toward business executives who were visiting for work. Rent per month was around $4000 CAD. After the departure of their latest tenant while they were living in Florida, a decision had been made to hire a real estate agent from a very large real estate brokerage to find them a tenant (property management would be taken care of by someone else). The agent was successful in finding them a tenant after a relatively brief search (the first warning sign for such an expensive property) and moved on to other business.

The tenant paid first and last months rent with a certified cheque. This would prove to be the only money our clients ever collected. On the second month, the tenant's cheque bounced. Then again on the third and fourth month. And after sending an eviction notice to the tenant (who was ignoring her completely) our client finally to reviewed the application the tenant had completed prior to moving in. It was around this time our office as contacted. A simple google search revealed that the company the tenant worked for did not exist, their credit report was fake, they had said they were the "personal director" at a company instead of "personnel director". These were errors that could have been detected with diligent search and investigation.

Our client's husband was in poor health and remained in Florida, but she flew back to Toronto to visit the unit. The tenant refused her entry, so she hired a locksmith and with police escort entered the unit upon giving adequate notice.

The living room had a quarter inch of water sitting on top of the hardwood. It has been sitting there for weeks. All of the hardwood in the property had become warped. The unit was filthy --- kitchen destroyed and half of the furniture *removed*. The damage to the unit, our clients source of retirement income for her and her family was over $90,000 dollars not mention the missing rent.

The tenant was a professional/predatory tenant who had been evicted nearly a dozen times before. A google search of the tenants real name revealed multiple stories written about her behavior.

We sued the real estate agent and the brokerage, but the landlord was not even close to being made whole. There are thousands of such cases each year. Your real estate agent isn't there to just **find** you a tenant, they are there to help you **screen** for a tenant. When they've found you someone, be sure to follow up and ask them why that person is acceptable and how they **verified** whatever information was submitted on their application. If the sole purpose of your agent is to receive applications and show the unit, that is a near useless service.

4. Do not be alone with tenants that have made threats toward you or appear mentally unstable. If you are a male and the tenant is female, endeavor to never be alone with them at all, ever.

One of our clients was accused of sexual harassment by his tenant. She used this accusation (never filed a complaint with the police) at the Landlord and Tenant Board as a reason to deny him access to the property while she was present. She was also in significant arrears of rent. We discovered through research that this same tenant had made similar accusations against multiple previous landlords. This accusation hurt him professionally and personally. He was eventually vindicated by the tenant's boyfriend, who I suppose, for whatever reason, decided to change his story upon cross examination.

Do not put yourself in situations where it will be your word against the word of a tenant who may have mental health issues. If you are being accused of anything that even has a whiff of physical contact to it, ensure you are never alone when attending the unit. Bring your wife or husband, a buddy, a friend, turn your cell on and record it -- whatever, protect yourself.

Advertising Your Tenancy

Quick Checklist

> - **Pictures.**
>
> - **A good description of the unit**
>
> - **Always remember to mention the proximity of key factors like schools, public transit and employers.**
>
> - **Competitive price.**

Do not pay for advertisements unless absolutely necessary

Advertising in a newspaper or placing a classified advertisement when where you are required to pay is a poor use of resources. A majority of prospective tenants find their units for rent on the internet.

These websites are everywhere. The bottom line is, you should generally not be paying to list your units. And if you are paying, that fee should be very low.

It is also good practice to have a sign advertising your vacancy outside of your unit for public display. People walking around the area are a great source of potential tenants and signs can be obtained cheaply.

Ensure that quality photographs are part of your advertisements

Most prospective tenants will ignore ads that do not post pictures of the rental unit. Take bright photographs and try to have the unit empty. Empty units look larger when pictures of them are taken. Also, if you are painting the unit prior to viewing, use white or off white paint. White paint, in addition to making the unit look brighter, makes it look bigger. Take pictures of the bathroom, living room and bedroom. Female tenants tend to care more about the condition of bathrooms and male tenants the living room.

Understand your customer

If your rental unit is close to a university, college, major employer or public transportation hub, make this clear in the headline of the posted ad. Prospective tenants spend only a few seconds browsing, so make your headline highlight the variables that add value to your unit.

Example:

<u>Bright & Spacious 1 Bedroom Apartment, minutes from Carleton and Ottawa Universities - $800</u>

Notes: Bright Spacious 1 bedroom basement apartment located on St. Francis near Gladstone.

> The apartment is newly renovated (counters, floors, freshly painted) with eat- in kitchen, very large windows and on-site laundry. Very nice area with many young professionals.
>
> Fridge, stove, heat and water included. Hydro extra. Parking available if necessary.
>
> MOVE - IN BONUS being offered. Email to find out more.

-OR-

These advertisements would be accompanied by photographs. What you want is the potential tenant to 'click' on your ad to begin with. For this you need something to the point and easy to read. Tenants want to know three basic things:

1) How much?
2) How nice?
3) Where?

Address these three questions as briefly as possible in your advertisement.

Also, we cannot enough stress the importance of "FOR RENT" signs in front of your rental unit. The best people to advertise to are people who already live in the neighborhood and are looking to move.

Pricing

Before advertising your unit for rent perform some market research. Look online at similar units and if you have the time, view them. Price your unit accordingly. The market can swing significantly, so it is important to be attentive to what is a competitive price in your neighborhood for a similar space. Remember, nothing is worse than vacancies – they will ruin the profitability of your investment.

Designing Your Lease

Quick Checklist

> - **Utilities included or excluded?**
>
> - **What amenities (parking est.) are included in rent?**
>
> - **Fixed term tenancy or month to month?**

Should utilities be included?

Deciding whether not to include utilities in your lease is an important decision. Our general advice is to rent units with utilities included. This is so that if the tenant fails to pay the utility bill, you can have them evicted as it is included in the cost of their rent. Obviously this is not always possible, but you should be made aware of the risk you undertake with some utility expenses. This is most usually a problem with **water bills.**

Water bills can be dangerous and you as a landlord may not discover your tenant is abusing water (leaving toilets running) or that there is a serious water issue until you receive a massive bill. Some tenants will attempt to punish landlords by ensuring that the water in their units keep running (toilets are particularly vulnerable to this) so be vigilant. Ensure their flushing mechanisms are in proper order and keep an eye on your monthly bill. It is very easy to engineer a constantly running toilet in order to generate a **ruinous** water bill.

Month to month tenancy vs. Fixed term tenancy

You have the option of making your lease week to week, month to month, year to year or for a fixed term of whatever length you choose. We generally recommend a lease for a term of **nothing longer than a year**. This is advantageous for two main reasons:

1. You have the freedom to increase rent on a yearly basis.

Provincial or State legislation controls when and for how much you can increase rent. In Ontario, for example, rent can be increased only once a year and for a prescribed percentage determined by the government. If you enter into a lease agreement of more than one year your rent will be frozen at the agreed amount. Even if your lease has a clause requiring rent to increase year over year that increase could be considered illegal.

2. You can more easily evict.

The process of eviction is legislated in each Province and State. Generally speaking, if the tenants lease has expired more grounds of eviction are available to you as a landlord. A tenancy that begins well may not end that way, and the year long lease gives you the opportunity to consider whether or not the tenant is a good fit for your unit.

Do not sign a residential lease for a term longer than 1 year and be highly suspicious of tenants who request a rental term of two years or longer. Tenants who have been evicted before try to sign lease contracts for abnormally long periods.

Offers to pay rent in advance

Be highly suspicious of offers to pay full rent months in advance. This the behavior of many undesirable tenants. Demanding rent to be paid months in advance is illegal in many jurisdictions and even if the tenant offers to do so. We have seen it used as a strategy by tenants who claim the rent was collected via extortion. And either way, in many jurisdictions, rent collected early must be returned, regardless of the circumstances in which it was given. We have had cases where a landlord accepted six months' rent in advance (as was offered by the tenant) and then the tenant claimed that the advanced rent was extorted from them in order to secure the unit. Save yourself the trouble. *It is highly suspicious and irregular for a tenant to offer you months of rent ahead of time.*

It is also irrational, as the funds could be used for something else in the interim. Be suspicious of irrational behavior such as this – if someone has a year's rent saved up why on Earth would they give it to you? Did they save it up because they had not been paying rent to their previous landlord for six months? This is frequently the case.

Property Maintenance

Quick Checklist

- **Inspection report**
- **Monthly inspections**
- **A Maintenance Book for any required repairs**

Inspect your unit on a bi-monthly basis (every two months). Regular inspections are important for a number of reasons. First, if utilities are included in rent, it's important to make sure household units that consume water are functioning correctly before your receive a massive bill. One experience we had was a landlord whose tenant's toilet broke (the water ran continually) but he never considered it worth reporting. He wasn't trying to hurt his landlord, he just didn't care that his toilet was running 24 hours a day, 7 days a week, 365 days a year. Tenants do not think the way a homeowner would; if they are not paying utilities they *do not care* about the conservation of those utilities. Checking for water leaks or the efficiency of items using utilities and inspecting on a regular basis is a key part of being a good landlord.

Inspections are also important so you can keep an eye on what is going on in your unit. Is the tenant causing damage? How do you know if you never take a look? If a tenant is destroying your unit you want to evict them fast. Do not wait until they move out and you discover there to be a missing wall between a bedroom and bathroom (this actually happened with one of our clients) or other terrible damage.

Another reason for inspections is to deter drug dealers and marijuana growing operations ("Grow Ops"). Drug dealers have taken to renting homes, condominiums and even apartment buildings so that they can use them to grow marijuana indoors. We have handled multiple Grow Op cases and the damage to homes can be in the tens of thousands.

Choosing A Good Tenant

Quick Checklist

- Landlord reference
- Employment check
- Credit check
- Proper screening

Telephone screening of prospective new tenants

The screening process for your prospective tenants should begin the moment you receive a phone call asking for a viewing appointment. The manner in which you deny a tenant housing must be done intelligently – and the earlier this screening is done, the better.

We do not advocate or condone discrimination for frivolous reasons such as race or gender, and people who engage in such practices pay a financial price as well as a legal one. However, in our view, some discriminating behavior that most people would consider reasonable is prohibited because of draconian pro-tenant legislation. In some jurisdictions, for example, 'no pet' provisions in leases are illegal. So even if you have a tenant who has agreed to not allow a pet into the home, if they breach this provision of their lease or lie to your face about their ownership of a pet, you cannot evict them for this contractual breach. Always be certain to ask the following of prospective tenants over the phone:

> *Take careful notes as you will later check these answers against testimony from their former landlord.*

Do they have pets?

Well managed pets are usually not a problem, but pets that are not cleaned up after can cause thousands of dollars in damage to a unit – damage that is particularly disgusting to repair. If they do have a pet, insist on meeting the pet before they move in. It may sound silly, but a small dog is only a small problem. A large Doberman moving into your basement and barking all night will significantly increase the stress in your life.

How many people will be living in the unit?

You will want to know how many people will be living on your property. This is a particularly important consideration if your rent has utilities included. Additional inhabitants consume additional electricity and water, costing you more money. There are also health and safety concerns. <u>Our standard lease requests the tenant to write down all 'occupants' of the home, which is useful in addressing this problem should eviction be necessary.</u> Some tenants will illegally sublet your unit to someone else or try and move in additional parties to pay for rent.

Why are you moving?

If your prospective tenant is moving because they've been evicted or some other nefarious reason it is highly unlikely they will tell you. Answers that take too long to deliver or are inarticulate should arouse suspicion. If the tenant was moving because he or she was looking for a place closer to work, the conversation may go something like this:

Why are you moving?

"I'm looking for a place closer to work." Where do you work?

"I work at the Government building on Preston"

Now you can verify their claim. Is their place of work closer to your unit then their prior home was? Did they answer you without hesitation? Asking the question and taking notes helps you assess credibility.

If someone is being deceptive the conversation may be:

Why are you moving?

"Uh, I uh, I'm just looking for a new place." What's wrong with your old place?

"I'm just looking for a new place, tired of my old home. Looking for a change"

Nobody enjoys moving. Moving is a hassle. Very few people are so odd as to be moving because they are 'looking for a change'. Answers such as this should arouse suspicion.

There is no sure fire way of telling when someone is lying to you, but if you record their answers and check them later against what their landlord says, you'll catch most people who try to deceive you.

One great tactic is to purposely misstate details given to you by the tenant to their prior landlord.

Have you given your Landlord proper notice?

Tenants are required to provide landlords proper notice before they can vacate their unit. This varies by province and state. The appropriate time is usually 60 days. If your prospective tenant has not given their prior landlord notice, they will not give you notice. It is also an interesting question because it tells you something about their relationship with their prior landlord. If they are on good terms with one another, there is no reason they will not have provided notice.

Preventing 'no shows'

Always collect a phone number from your prospective tenant prior to scheduling their appointment. Confirm the appointment with them an hour or so before to ensure they will be there. You would be amazed how often tenants will cancel and not contact you. Also, schedule appointments five minutes apart – this way you will be able to have viewings quickly and move on with your day. Also, it will appear as though there is significant interest in your unit when your phone rings and you have to grab another prospective tenant. The appearance of interest pressures tenants to agree to rent with you. Have application forms ready for tenants to complete when they arrive at the building for a showing.

Do not stop showing the unit to potential tenants until a lease has been signed <u>and</u> a deposit collected

Until you have collected a deposit from someone do not stop showing the unit. People will often tell you 'they'll take it' only to cancel later after they see another place. Once you have collected a deposit (one month's rent) do not return it if they change their mind. Make them aware that the deposit is non- refundable. If they complain, tell them that you turned down other people who were interested in the unit because you had accepted their deposit. Always keep the deposit.

Employment Check

An employment check is in our view the most important part of determining whether or not to rent to a prospective tenant. Many people make a great deal of noise about credit checks, and they are an important part of checking prospective tenants, but they are useless in evaluating a significant number of people and sometimes a waste of money. Credit checks, remember, do not take into account income. Being lawyers, we frequently meet people after the tenant relationship has broken down and they are trying to evict the tenant, or be compensated for loss of rental income or damage to their home. When trouble occurs, you need to know where your tenants work. This is because you need to be able to garnish their income if they refuse to pay you. Many landlords do not think, when starting a tenancy, of what they will do if they are owed thousands of dollars or their home is damaged. If you win your case in court, how do you collect? Verifying employment (and keeping the employment record up to date) is your ultimate insurance. If you know where they work, they cannot run unless they also run from their employer. Also, garnishing someone's wage is very embarrassing. Tenants will often pay what they owe if you only threaten to contact their employer with a court order to garnish their wages. It also keeps tenants honest; as they would prefer to not be embarrassed at work

Employment verification is also important because you can confirm their income. As a general rule, rent should be no more than 35% of your tenant's income. So if your rent is $1000 a month, your tenant's income should be no less than $3500 a month. Otherwise you increase significantly the chances of their occasional default. You should also verify their employment to determine its nature and duration. If they will be losing the job in three months or if it is seasonal, you need to know. You also need to verify (if they are paid on an hourly basis) their hourly wage and the typical number of hours per week they are given. Check all of this information against what your prospective tenant told you on their application to determine their honesty.

Credit Checks

Credit checks are an important part of your toolbox to determine whether or not a potential tenant is suitable to rent your unit. Credit checks do however cost money, so if they can be avoided, we recommend you do so. If you can afford it, narrow down the number of potential renters to a reasonable number and then only check the credit of those you consider seriously.

It's important to understand what a credit check tells you - simply put, a credit check tells you how prompt a potential tenant is in paying their creditors – that's it. The only reason these checks are assumed to be of use is because of the presumption that there exists a correlation between how conscientiously a tenant pays their creditor and how conscientious they will be in paying you. There is often a correlation, and we do recommend credit checks – but be careful. Many good tenants have bad credit and credit checks are ineffective on a few types of tenants. We do not recommend credit checks when dealing with the following potential tenants (they are usually a waste of money):

1. Immigrants;
2. Students;
3. Anyone below the age of 30.

'Self-employed' or on Social Assistance (welfare)

The best way to avoid tenant problems is to avoid problem tenants. There are certain types of tenants that are frequently problematic – namely, those who are 'self-employed' or on social assistance. It is important to remember that unlike other sources of income, social assistance **cannot be garnished** so if your tenant fails to pay rent or causes damage, you have no recourse in terms of taking their income. 'Self-employment' is usually an inconsistent provider of income. Sure, there are some tenants who are 'self-employed' and will pay their rent on time every time, but being 'self-employed' reduces this probability. Investigate their self-employment. 'Construction' is by far in our experience the worst kind of 'self-employment' and the least consistent. Rent to these people with extreme care.

Some government programs pay landlords directly on behalf of tenants. **Beware, many of these programs will cancel their direct payments to you should the tenant request it.**

Renting to students

<u>Always have a guarantor.</u> The guarantor should be investigated to the same extent you would investigate a potential tenant. Be sure you find out where the guarantor works, their address and other pertinent contact information. Remember, your mind should be geared towards what you would need to do in the event that the student could not pay rent or damaged your property. You need to make sure you can find and if necessary, take to court, the guarantor. You also want to make sure the guarantor is responsible <u>cares about their</u> <u>reputation</u> and has a legitimate connection to the student.

In our experience guarantors that are 'friends', or 'aunts and uncles' are warning signs that something is not right. The guarantors that have been great for us have usually been parents. Mothers or fathers make great guarantors, in particular mothers or fathers who are reputation conscious. This is a more difficult thing to tease out, but if people care about their reputation they will be more willing to pay you if their child damages your property. Typically, reputation conscious people are those that are more educated or members of professions: lawyers, doctors, people working for government, accountants or engineers.

Some students are much more trouble than others. We've made this list in descending order of reliability:

Graduate Students

We have never had a graduate student fail to pay rent on time or cause our clients significant problems. Whatever the reason, these make good tenants.

Undergraduate university Students

Make sure you have a guarantor, but University students are less likely to be problems. Their guarantors are also more likely to be reputation conscious. We have had very few problems with University students.

College Students

We have had numerous problems with college students, be it property damage, consistent late payment of rent or people who 'move in' and try to sublet without permission. As a general rule the less serious the program of study the less you want to rent to these tenants. Investigate guarantors thoroughly.

Renting to friends

You don't really know someone until you've lived in close proximity to them. Sometimes a friendship really shouldn't be allowed to step outside the boundaries of beers and golf. Few things are worse than having to take legal action against a "friend" for nonpayment or destruction of property. Unless you've previously lived with, or near, a responsible friend that would provide for a solid tenant, it may be best in this situation to find a reliable stranger to rent the space to.

Renting to recent immigrants

Just as with students, recent immigrants do not usually have an extensive credit history. In our experience, recent immigrants make very good tenants, as many have **a heightened fear of possible eviction** and are uneducated about laws in place to protect them from hostile landlords. Our most serious predatory tenants are with few exceptions all Canadian born – well aware of their 'rights' – and by those we mean, their ability to frustrate legitimate evictions and manipulate the legal system.

Renting to tenants who have bad credit

Many people who cannot purchase a home usually have this problem because of poor credit from some financial event earlier in their lives. It would be unwise to dismiss people who meet other criteria simply because of their credit rating. Also, particularly in an environment of low interest rates, a larger and larger proportion of people renting larger homes or expensive condos will be part of this latter group. These folks can be good tenants.

Guarantors

Guarantors are parties who sign a lease in addition to the primary tenant and promise to pay you rent should the primary tenant default. Guarantors are responsible for complete payment of the lease and all the same obligations as the tenant. When renting to students a guarantor is strongly recommended. They can also be used when renting to tenants whose income or references suggest they may default on rent. You should be certain to verify the Guarantor is capable of paying the rent should they be required to. Obtain employment verification from the guarantor so you can garnish their wages if necessary.

Google the tenants name and employer

We have had clients whose tenants were notorious for defrauding landlords. One in particular had an article written about her by the Toronto Star. There were numerous newsgroups dedicated to warning landlords about this individual. Had the landlord 'Googled' her name, she would have discovered this information and saved over $30,000 worth of damages to her home. Some tenants will also submit bogus employment information. A simple Google search can confirm the address and phone number of the company for whom they claim to work. You'll be surprised how much a five minute search online can verify.

Go to where they currently live to have your lease signed

Try and have the lease signed where the tenants currently reside. Plan to meet them at their home to sign the lease – this way you get to see how they currently live before agreeing to have them live in your unit. It is also useful for you to offer to 'drop off' application papers at their home to take a quick look at the property. If on your arrival you see something that is extremely disturbing, drive away.

The tenant with the sad story…

Do not fall for sad stories, 'charm', hard times or whatever other fantasy you might hear from a perspective tenant. We cannot count the number of problems that begin this way.

Make an intelligent cold business decision and you will be far less likely to have problems.

Once A New Tenant Moves In

Quick Checklist

- Pictures of what the unit looks like when they move in.

- Inspection checklist.

- Repair checklist.

- Rent receipts .

Document Everything

When the tenant moves in take pictures of what the unit looked like the moment they moved in. Have them sign and complete an inspection checklist, where anything that needs to be repaired is noted. Tenants will frequently claim in court that damages in a unit were 'present when they moved in' or some other nonsense in order to defraud you. Protect yourself and your property by documenting what the unit looked like the day they moved in.

Issue rent receipts and keep good records

When a tenant pays their rent give them a receipt. Ideally, give them a receipt they are required to sign. Keep a copy of the receipt for your records. When a tenant pays partial rent, give them a receipt for the portion they paid with a notation for 'partial rent', or whatever circumstance accounts for the missing/surplus money. Consider; what do you do if the tenant claims they paid you rent when they did not? Or claim you have 'forgotten' about a payment they made at one time or another? What is your proof you were paid? Where are your records? Evidence of a deposit into your business account may not be entirely convincing. Keeping receipts will keep you out of trouble. Do not accept cash unless you are also giving them a receipt for the cash.

Do not accept 'repair work' or any other sort of labour in lieu of rent.

This is a very common landlord mistake. We have participated in innumerable cases of litigation where the landlord made a verbal or written agreement with a tenant for them to conduct some miscellaneous repair in exchange for a rent discount. Inevitably, the 'repair work' is either done incorrectly or not at all and the rent is then not paid. The tenant then claims the repair has been done and they don't owe you the rent. The Courts are then forced to adjudicate whether or not the repairs have been completed, and trust me; they will not usually side with you, regardless of the facts. Rent is rent, period. If you have repairs you want completed, that is a separate contract with your tenant. It has nothing, whatsoever, to do with rent.

Here is an example:

> *Tenant Steve offers to make repairs to Unit 3 of your building as well as his unit if you decrease his rent from $800 to $500 for three months. You agree to his terms, but have him sign the same standard lease for $800 a month. You then sign a **separate contract** with Steve saying you will pay him $300 each month for three months in compensation for work being performed should it meet your standards. In this way, should the repairs be substandard or anything else occur, your rent is contractually a separate issue. Steve is welcome to take you to Small Claims court should he think you have not paid him fairly but he cannot cease paying you rent.*

Ensure your tenant is not fixing issues that are significantly impair his ability to enjoy the rental unit, or the issues he/she is 'fixing' may become the subject of a maintenance complaint.

Terminating A Tenancy

Terminating a tenancy can be a very complicated affair and there are many grounds for termination. For fear of turning this guide into an encyclopedia, we've included only the three most common reasons a landlord seeks to evict someone. Regardless of the legal jurisdiction, the same excuses are routinely made.

Non-Payment of Rent

What your tenant will claim:
1. They will claim they never received your non-payment of rent notice (or whatever you are required to deliver in your legal jurisdiction).

In Ontario, the legal document you must deliver is a N4 - Notice of Termination for Non Payment of Rent. If you deliver your N4 notice alone, take a picture of the notice being slid underneath the tenant's door or placed in their mailbox. If you mail the letter, keep a receipt of the mailing and do not use regular mail. Use a mailing service where you can track receipt of the letter -- not personal receipt of the letter, but confirmation it has been dropped off at the address. We do not suggest you insist up on a signature. If the tenant refuses to sign the package it will not be delivered and their refusal does not constitute service in many legal jurisdictions. You want confirmation the letter arrived at the address, not that the tenant signed for it. Predatory tenants will simply not pick up registered letters you send them.

2. They will claim they never received the Notice of Hearing

Use the same strategy for preventing this claim as you did for the late rent notice. You may have an eviction for non-payment of rent hearing and the tenant does not appear. This is frequently done on purpose, with the tenant subsequently claiming for whatever reason, the Notice of Hearing never arrived at their home.

3. They will make an excuse to reschedule or delay the Hearing

Predatory tenants know that if they can ask for the hearing to be rescheduled for whatever ridiculous reason (as they have no intention of paying you) it will mean they have significantly more time in the rental unit. The tribunal in most rental jurisdictions are usually very busy. The next available hearing dates are frequently months away. If this request occurs, tell the adjudicator why such a request would be unfairly prejudicial to you. Explain the hardship you are going through because of the missing rent and what it has cost you in human terms. If the adjudicator grants the reschedule, ask for it to be 'preemptory'. A preemptory hearing is one that cannot once more be rescheduled. Decisions such as this are almost entirely at the discretion of the decision maker. You will need to appeal to that discretion.

4. They will claim you are lying to the Tribunal about whether rent was paid.

This is why you need to keep good receipts and records. They will sometimes claim they 'sent you cheques' and you simply choose not to cash them. This is a frequent claim from tenants who are in the habit of giving you checks that bounce. Show your records to discount this claim, and if they claim cheques were sent, demand to know when they were sent and ask them to produce records of the cheques being cashed.

5. They will claim there exists some agreement that changes the amount of rent they should be paying.

Never enter into any agreement changing the amount of rent owed on your lease, especially if this suggestion is brought to you by a tenant offering their 'services' to repair something. If your tenant makes this claim at a hearing, ask for evidence of this agreement. The story should appear false in the face of your records.

6. They will claim that some kind of damage or maintenance issue in the unit means they shouldn't have to pay you full rent.

This one is a favorite of predatory tenants. They will find some kind of damage in the home (often damage they create themselves) and then claim that this damage means they should receive something called a 'rent abatement' (money subtracted) from the monthly rent. This is a very common tactic to both delay the hearing (as it takes significant time for the tenant to explain the damage and the 'suffering' they are enduring because of it) and to try and cheat you out of your full rent. This is why you need to have an inspection report when the tenant moves in. I cannot stress enough how many landlords have been ruined by tenants who engage in this strategy. Predatory tenants will cause damage to your property, call building inspectors or city officials and do their best to ruin you. Protect yourself with images of your home when the tenant moved in (that they sign off on) and consistent inspections. Have records of any claims of maintenance issues (and your efforts to repair them) prepared ahead of time.

Termination for Damage to the Unit

A landlord may give a tenant this notice if the tenant, another occupant of the rental unit or a person whom the tenant permits in the residential complex willfully or negligently causes undue damage to the rental unit or residential complex. In Ontario this notice is called N5 - Notice to End your Tenancy for Interfering with Others, Damage or Overcrowding. The precise nomenclature will vary by province and state.

What your tenant will claim:
1. They will claim that they never received any of your notices (N5 or the Notice of Hearing).

As with before, ensure you have proof the notices were delivered.

2. They will claim the damage you are blaming them for was in place when they moved into the apartment.

This is why it is important to take pictures of the unit before a tenant moves in. It is also important to have a tenant complete an inspection report where they admit what deficiencies, if any, exist in the unit. If you did not take pictures when the tenant moved in, try and bring with you to the hearing someone who saw the apartment before the tenant moved in who can attest to its prior condition.

3. They will claim you are exaggerating the damage.

It may seem hard to believe, but some landlords arrive at a hearing with nothing other than their words describing damage to their property. Bring pictures, video and any other evidence of the damage you are complaining about. Bring three copies, one for you, one for the judge and one for the tenant. If you have spent money to have your unit repaired, bring the receipts. If you have not repaired the damage but plan to, bring an estimate from a repair company to substantiate the amount of money you are asking for.

3. They will claim the damage is the result of ordinary use

Tenants are not expected to pay you for damage accruing from ordinary use of the unit – things like worn down stairs or chipped paint. Make sure you can establish that the damage was not only caused by them, but was also not caused by ordinary use of the unit. If the stairs were torn off, have a workman or someone with expert knowledge write you a letter saying that in their experience the damage caused must have been from abuse or the tenants behavior (which is not ordinary).

Terminating a tenancy for the Landlords Own Use (or someone is purchasing the unit)

Landlords in Ontario and other jurisdictions are permitted to give notice of termination to a tenant if the landlord, in good faith, requires the unit for residential occupation by: the landlord, the landlord's spouse; a child or a parent of either the landlord or the landlord's spouse; or a person who provides or will provide care services to the landlord or a family member of the landlord where the person receiving care services resides or will reside in the building. This notice can also be given if the property is being sold and the buyer needs to move in.

Many landlords complete this form incorrectly and have their applications thrown out as a result. The most common error in Ontario is one of an incorrect termination date, the requirements for this eviction ground vary province to province and state to state. If you are evicting a tenant for this reason, particularly if you are selling the property, hire a legal professional to ensure you are able to give the buyer vacant possession of your unit. Do not do this yourself unless absolutely necessary in the aforementioned circumstances.

What your tenant will claim:

1. They never received your notices (N12 or Notice of Hearing).

We've gone over how to handle this one in our other examples.

2. They will claim your notice is on bad faith

In this case, your tenant is essentially saying that you are lying to the board and have no intention of moving into the unit for the reason specified. Many landlords use N12 (the Ontario version of this notice) notices to evict troublesome tenants and have no intention to move into the property. For this reason the Board reviews carefully these applications.

If you are evicting the tenant because a loved one is moving into the home, have them appear before the tribunal to testify. If they can't appear to testify, have them complete an affidavit explaining why they need to move into the unit. The explanation must be credible. For example, if your daughter seeks to move into the unit, she can write in an affidavit:

> *"I currently live at________. I would like to move into the unit located on ________street because it is closer to my university and I will be able to study and go to work far easier. I have every intention of living in________and this application is being made in good faith. I cannot attend the hearing in person today because of__"*

If you are selling the home to someone and they wish to live in the unit, you still need to have them either appear at the hearing or complete an affidavit. You also need to bring with you proof that the home has been sold. Usually an Agreement of Purchase and Sale is sufficient.

If you have given your tenant any other forms for eviction in recent history **you will need to be extra diligent in convincing the Board that your request is genuine.** Have an explanation for why you gave the tenant those other forms. The Board will suspect you are using the N12 application to evict the tenant when you failed to do so for other reasons.

Basic Ways the Law Is Stacked Against Landlords

	Tenants	Landlords
Disclosure	Names and addresses of any landlord who has made a filing with the Landlord and Tenant Board is available for a fee.	Landlords don't have access to any eviction records.
Legal Representation	Any tenant, regardless of their income, is automatically qualified for free legal advice and representation.	Landlords are expected to "know" what is required of them, how to prepare legal documents, how to represent themselves, or retain paid representation.
Security	Don't have to pay security deposits to cover any damage if they destroy the place (varies per jurisdiction).	Cannot deduct damage from tenants last month's rent (their only form of security).
Fees	Tenants wishing to bring their landlord to the landlord tenant board only pay a minimum of fees.	A landlord wishing to bring a matter before the Board pays significantly higher fees.
Discretion	Tenants will almost always receive the benefit of the doubt when a decision	Landlords are presumed to be powerful and have the

	comes down to the decision makers discretion.	capacity to make correct decisions. When discretion is exercised, it is usually against your interest. "We'll give the tenant some time to pay instead of evicting them" for example.

Common Landlord Mistakes

- **If you will be seeking eviction of a tenant for multiple reasons file all applications at the same time, that way you can often avoid multiple application fees.** This was before COVID when applications were made in person. It is possible this entire system may be moved online.

- **Collect as much information as possible from prospective tenants before they move in.**

All of the information you collect in the process of deciding on a tenant should be collected with the protection of your residential asset (you home or building) in mind. If the tenant damages your property or suddenly moves out, how will you find them? Where do they Bank? What is the address of their employer? How long have they been working there? In order to obtain a judgement against a tenant in Small Claims Court you will need to know this information.

Document everything

Document all of your correspondence with tenants; all of your emails, letters and even conversations. There is no need to record entire conversations in painful details, just make a brief note of what was discussed and when. This record will be invaluable when things go wrong.

When someone is in arrears of rent serve them with a notice of late payment as soon as possible.

All eviction processes begin when your tenant has been properly served a notice of eviction. If you do not file this notice immediately upon the late or non-payment of your rent the earliest date that you may have your tenant evicted moves forward. <u>This does not mean you are required to evict the</u> <u>tenant,</u> it simply allows you to evict them, should you choose to do so at an earlier date. It is not correct to simply 'paste the notice on your tenant's door', you must comply with the requirements outlined in the Residential Tenancies Act in Ontario (or your local legislation). Hand the notice to them in person, slide it under their door or put it in their mailbox.

As a part of your lease, have a fee that is charged to deliver notices of any kind.

Some tenants habitually pay rent as late as possible, only giving you payment when they have been served a notice for late payment of rent (N4). This is a waste of your time and slows your rental income. An administration fee for serving forms can be adequate disincentive to renters to keep you waiting at the start of the month. Contact us about the legal requirements of such a fee. You may also evict someone for persistent late payment of rent.

Not following proper legal procedure when deciding to evict a tenant.

Landlords who do not follow the proper legal procedure when evicting a tenant pay severe penalties that can run into the thousands of dollars. This does not include what your tenant may be costing you by damaging your property and costing you rental income. Follow the legal steps no matter how tedious.

Evicting tenants during the winter is twice as difficult! If you want them out, do it in when the weather is good.

Decision makers in many jurisdictions are given a significant amount of discretion when it comes to evicting a tenant. They can essentially deny the eviction for near any reason, with errors only being corrected upon review or even worse, on appeal to a higher court. If you are going to evict a tenant its best to do it when it is warm.

Do not change the locks on the doors until you have legal authority to do so.

Until the tenant has been evicted by the Sheriff you do not have the authority to change the locks on the doors.

A client volunteered to write this for us, we decided to include it in this work for its honesty and candor:

Property management without tears: My personal journey as a landlord

Successfully managing a property is challenging because you must continue to create economic value in all you do. In my experience, three factors appeared to be the most important predictor of success: finding good tenants; managing the on-going landlord-tenant relationship; making sure that you are flexible enough to make good decisions that keep you in the black.

Like many people, I approached property management with trepidation because I imagined that it would involve dealing with tenancy laws and tenant issues, loss of personal time and unimaginable grief. In time, all these concerns were fully realized. On the positive side, I have always believed that few people will take as much interest in my financial success as I do. And, there was no turning back, because I could not afford to hire a property management firm and I needed to grow. Here is my story.

I have been a landlord for 10 years. Starting out, I managed one single home. Over the years the properties I manage have increased to include several homes and two multiplexes. At the beginning, the first task was to be knowledgeable about the landlord - tenant laws in my particular jurisdiction and secure applicable forms and leases that are detailed and comprehensive. As well, I read real estate management books, and subscribed to a landlord advisory service for back-up on issues that needed clarification and advice. By the end of my second year as a landlord, I started feeling that I had good control and knowledge over many matters. Furthermore, it was helpful to establish a relationship with an efficient landlord whose practices and knowledge I respected and who I chatted with from time to time. Perhaps the biggest source of strength in the early years was when it dawned on me that immediately after I chose a good tenant, I should calmly focus on the landlord-tenant relationship and how you progress with each step.

Here's how I tried to create value in my business:

1. at all times

- Create an effective rent roll / rent tracking system and have access to landlord tenant forms. Whenever necessary ensure that you serve appropriate forms/ give notices to tenants on time, in order to minimize economic loss. Also, any agreement with tenants outside the lease must be written agreements, duly signed by both parties.

- Use web sites with good traffic for low cost advertising and place street signs. Use expensive advertisement only as a last resort.

- Keep your rents in line with rents for comparable properties in the general area, to promote stability in tenancy.

2. Finding new tenants

- Be patient and selective. Finding good tenants is as time consuming as evicting old tenants.

- You should use websites to save on costs unless your rental property area has unique characteristics that cause you to use newspaper ads.

- Schedule rental appointments in bunches, with 10-15 minute intervals. You save time/money and a string of prospective tenants causes other potential tenants in line to make a quick commitment, thinking that they may lose out on something.

- Always carry rental application forms with you or have an easy way of emailing prospective tenants a copy of the form.

- Because it is allowed in the jurisdiction where I rent (Ontario), I encourage tenants to attach a last month's rent cheque to their applications. If their application is successful I will cash the cheque immediately. The last months deposit cheque is non-refundable and I clearly state this in my receipt to the prospective tenant.

<u>Some deceptive practices that may cost you dearly</u>

- Giving false previous landlord references. When verifying references call the 'pervious landlord' and speak to with them in a casual manner asking general questions before you get to what you really want to know. If you are clever you can usually tell when the person you are speaking to is not really a landlord. This also makes them either nervous or more comfortable with you, both of which make it easier to notice deception.

- If all references check out arrange a meeting with the prospective tenant at the house where they **currently live**. This need not be done overtly, you may simply tell them you will 'drive to their home' to have them sign additional papers. If you do not like their house keeping habits do not rent to them.

- Be friendly but maintain distance and professionalism at all times in your relations with tenants in order to be able to enforce your rules.

- Be wary of late payments, as the lateness tends to increase over time if it is not dealt with. Your tenant will get into the habit of giving you late rent is you accept them routinely without giving the tenant some kind of penalty. You may issue a notice to pay rent form as a first step towards possible eviction whenever late is rent, however when possible a friendly request may be more appropriate. If rent is late more than once deliver the late payment notice. Do not approach the problem in a casual or cavalier manner.

- Stop payment by cheque once a tenant's cheque bounces more than once. After this accept only cash. This condition should be written in your lease.

- Before a tenant moves in take a picture of the inside of the unit and property so that you may show (if need be) a judge or arbitrator its condition prior to occupation.

3. Keeping Good Tenants

- - When small problems arise, respond to the tenants requests and notify them if there are delays.

- You must maintain control at all times and ensure that you maintain professional relationships.

> *"Real Estate is the best investment in the world because it's the only thing they're not making anymore."*
>
> **— Will Rogers**

www.ingramcontent.com/pod-product-compliance
Lightning Source LLC
Chambersburg PA
CBHW031919270726
48655CB00006BA/2819